CENTENNIAL HISTORY

of

MACEDONIA LUTHERAN

CHURCH

1869–1969

Larry W. Fuqua

PREFACE

"History", it has been said, "is an account of something which never happened, written by someone who wasn't there". Since the material in this book covers a period of many years, I cannot claim that the work contains no errors. Many sources have been consulted in preparing this material, and in some instances, it has been difficult to select the most plausible from a group of conflicting facts.

The purpose of this book is to provide a chronological picture of the historical advancement and achievements of Macedonia Lutheran Church and its people.

It is my hope that I have discolored no facts, misrepresented no events, nor failed to give as true and as accurate a picture of this congregation as possible. I appreciate the invaluable assistance of the Special Historical Committee appointed by the Church Council. These people are as follows: Mr. Daniel Apple, Mrs. Helen Bevan, Mr. Jeffrey Bond, Mrs. Eva Clemmer, Mr. George A. Keck, Mrs. Linda Irwin, Mrs. Lottie Murrie, Mrs. Beulah Sullivan and Miss Susan Whiteside.

Especially do I appreciate the work done by Mrs. Eva Clemmer in the previous history which was written in 1959. Also, I would like to give special recognition to Mrs. Beulah Sullivan and Pastor Whiteside for their assistance and encouragement on this project.

Larry W. Fuqua

2

TABLE OF CONTENTS

The founding of Macedonia Lutheran Church was not an isolated event. It was simply a step in the growth of the Lutheran Church in North Carolina, Alamance County and the Burlington Community. The need for a church naturally came to be as a result of the founding of Company Shops which later became Burlington. But we cannot begin with Company Shops or even with the older Lutheran Churches in our community for our roots are much deeper.

The story of Macedonia Lutheran Church and all Protestant churches began when Martin Luther, an Augustinian Monk in the Catholic Church, nailed his Ninety-five Theses on the door of the Wittenburg Castle Church on October 31, 1517, the eve of All Saint's Day. At this time Martin Luther had no idea of breaking away from the ancient church but unbeknown to him his actions had started a vast reform movement and he had founded what became the largest Protestant Church in the world. Also there followed a century and a half of religious wars and persecution.

German immigration to America grew out of the fearful results of these religious wars and persecution that left their country desolate and made existence there intolerable. The new world opened an asylum for these people. Thousands left their native land by way of England and Holland to reach a home in the wilderness. Most of these landed in Pennsylvania which for all practical purposes became a German colony.

During the period between 1768-1775 the archives of the colony of Pennsylvania record the names of more than 30,000 persons who landed at the port of Philadelphia. Many of these immigrants came to North Carolina as most of the valuable lands in Pennsylvania were taken up.

A goodly number of the Pennsylvania Dutch settled in what became Alamance County and neighboring territory. Those who settled in Alamance stopped on the fertile banks of the Great and Little Alamance and the Stinking Quarter Creeks as well as on the banks of the Haw River. Migrating in congregations in the 1740's most of these Germans were Lutherans. Ludwig Klapp's grant on the Alamance was issued in 1752. Michael Holt owned vast possessions along the Great and Little Alamance. John Faust had land on Cain Creek and Adam Trollinger on the west bank of Haw River, north of the present railroad crossing. Christian Foust, Jacob Albrect, Peter Sharp, Jacob Christman, and David Ephland were other pioneer Germans.[1]

These people had but little to do with the affairs of State because of their German language. They held no civil office, but

[1]Ruth Blackwelder, *The Age of Orange*, (Charlotte, 1961), p. 8.

they made good soldiers when the Cherokee Indians came against them. When called from their loom-making, cloth weaving, dairying, and agricultural pursuits during the Regulation Movement they went like a storm as farmers and men of the soil are wont to do when called upon to adjust such affairs.[2]

By 1773 so many Germans had migrated to western Orange that an English traveler had difficulty in finding persons west of Hillsborough who understood his language.[3]

These early settlers of Alamance not only brought their Bibles (we frequently run across these old German Bibles) but they had scarcely reared a log cabin and cleared a few acres of land when they began to build a schoolhouse that served as a place of worship.[4] After better days a more comfortable house of worship was reared but near it still stood the schoolhouse. The schoolmasters acted as ministers also in most cases. The first German Church was a log building near the present Low's Lutheran Church and the old Salisbury (Trading Path) Road. There two congregations worshipped together. The local schoolmaster, and occasionally a traveling preacher, read the scriptures to them in German. They sang together the hymns in the Gemeinschaftliche Gesanbuch. In some of the early union churches, Lutheran services were held one Sunday and Reformed Services the following Sunday.[5]

The present churches of Friedens and St. Paul's were originally union Lutheran and Reformed, but by 1771 Friedens had become wholly Lutheran and by 1801 St. Paul's had become wholly Lutheran.

These early churches such as Friedens, St. Paul's, Low's, Richland, Cobles, and Mount Pleasant were in existence many years and "doing a splendid job in their respective communities before there was any demand for a Lutheran Church in the Company Shops."[6]

As the result of an act passed by the Legislature of North Carolina in January 1849 the N. C. Railroad was incorporated. The railroad was to run from Goldsboro to Charlotte by way of Hillsboro, Greensboro, Salisbury, a distance of 223 miles.

---

[2]Sallie W. Stockard, *The History of Alamance County*, (Raleigh, 1900), pp. 78-79.

[3]John F. D. Smyth, *A Tour In The United States of America*, (2 vols., Dublin, 1784); I, p. 153.

[4]Stockard, *The History of Alamance County*, p. 78.

[5]Walter Whitaker, *Centennial History of Alamance County*, (Charlotte, 1949), p. 109.

[6]Eva Christman Clemmer, *History of Macedonia Lutheran Church*, (Burlington, 1959), p. 1.

General Benjamin Trollinger, who ran the cotton mill at Haw River, suggested that the road be constructed by his mill. He was willing to build the bridges which would be needed across the river. Several other influential men backed up his idea. The railroad must come through Alamance County, they said. And, so it did.

Before the first rails were laid, the North Carolina Railroad Company selected a location where they could build repair and maintenance shops. This location as well as an alternate location did not work out, for many people in Western Alamance did not want the railroad shops.

For the Railroad Company, this was insult added to injury. They decided to ignore these impertinent Alamancians. Maybe Greensboro would be better, at that. Had not Benjamin Trollinger come to the rescue at this point, the county might have lost the shops altogether. General Trollinger was a man of foresight. The railroad, he said, could build shops on his property two miles west of Graham. The offer was quickly accepted before the General could change his mind, and in his report to the stockholders in 1854, the Railroad President announced the choice.[7]

Besides General Trollinger's land, the railroad tract included the property of Nancy and Willis Sellars, Henry Tarpley, Steve Richardson, and James Fonville.[8]

The shops were finished in 1857 and the village had grown to twenty-seven buildings. Thirty-nine white men, twenty negro slaves and two free negroes were employed in or around the shops.[9]

The village of Company Shops continued to grow during the war years. The completion of several new buildings was announced in 1864 to the stockholders of the North Carolina Railroad.[10]

Company Shops was Incorporated in February 1866. The corporate limits of the town were specified to be a mile and one-half square, "having for the center of the same, the Hotel of the North Carolina Railroad."[11]

The first record of Lutherans in the Company Shops area was in 1869. It was "The Little Church In The Wildwood"[12] just west of what is now Elmira Street about where the Burlington Industries Mayfair Tricot Plant now stands under a

---

[7]Whitaker, *Centennial History of Alamance County*, p. 109.
[8]*Ibid*, 109.
[9]*Ibid*, 111.
[10]*Ibid*, 133.
[11]*Documents of the North Carolina Legislature*, (Raleigh, 1866).
[12]Julian Hughes, *Burlington Times News*, (March 29, 1956).

Macedonia

The Village of Burlington in 1890 with Macedonia Lutheran Church in the far background. Courtesy Egbert Riddle.

The congregation in 1894. Courtesy Mrs. Eva Clemmer.

8

brush arbor. This arbor was erected by just a few families under the leadership of layman Gideon L. Greeson who was the town and community schoolteacher. He was born and reared in the Low's Lutheran Church area some 10 or 11 miles west. He was the son of Solomon Greeson and the grandson of the Rev. Jacob Greeson. The year 1869 was when Ulysses S. Grant was inaugurated as President of the United States. At that time the only industry in this area to speak of was the North Carolina Railroad Shops. Consequently the congregation of the Lutheran Church in the wildwood waste of Company Shops consisted of only a few persons, including farmers of the neighborhood and some of the shophands. Quite likely the house of worship was an unpretentious log structure. In April, 1869, the same year the brush arbor church was constructed in the Oak Grove at Mayfair, these few pioneer citizens of Company Shops and vicinity petitioned the Synod which was in session in Friedens Lutheran Church near Gibsonville to establish a mission at this place, and assist them in support of a regular pastor.

The Synod granted the request and made the Rev. W. A. Julian the pastor. The transaction was at the regular session of the Synod, and a congregation was immediately organized. At a special session of the Synod held at Salem Lutheran Church, Rowan County, in August, 1869, Macedonia Lutheran Church, Company Shops, North Carolina was officially received into the Synod.

After Pastor Julian had served for about a year, and following a vacancy of three years until 1873, Simeon Scherer, who was pastor of Friedens Lutheran Church and perhaps Low's Lutheran Church, became the next pastor serving this parish for about three years.

In February of 1874, the North Carolina Railroad Company, which owned considerable land along their track through Company Shops, deeded six and ¾ acres of land near the center of the town and adjoining the railroad to a Board of Trustees, composed of W. L. Thorneburg, J. C. Holt, J. G. Moore, A. C. McAllister, and Daniel Worth for the purpose of a Union Church. After having used the brush arbor for five years the Lutheran Church moved into the newly built Union Church.

The Union Church was a two-story structure held together by wooden sills, sleepers, studding and beveled siding. The roof was covered with pine shingles and the windows had numerous glass panes that were a tempting target for boys who liked to throw rocks.

The Union Church which was the home of the congregation from 1874-1879. Courtesy Miss Lila Newman.

The first permanent home of the congregation 1879-1909.

The Lutheran Mission moved ahead in these early years, but progress was very slow just as it was in the town of Company Shops for these were the years of reconstruction, and there was much building and rebuilding to be done in this area as well as the rest of the nation.

In 1886 the North Carolina Railroad Company decided to transfer its operations to Manchester, Virginia, and the railroad offices and shops at Company Shops were closed.

With the removal of the business which had given the village its name, Company Shops threatened to become a ghost town. There were a few stores along Main Street, but most of the present business district consisted of vacant lots. Three cotton mills and the two-year old Burlington Coffin Factory were the only sizeable industries in the village.

Nevertheless, the Railroad Hotel still attracted salesmen and visitors, and, depending heavily on their infant industries and businesses to see them through to better times, the 1,000 to 1,500 inhabitants of Company Shops worked to keep the village alive.

In February, 1887, several of the town's leading citizens held a meeting for the purpose of selecting a more distinguished name for their town. These men, Dr. B. A. Sellars, Dr. R. A. Freeman, Captain James A. Turrentine, Joseph A. Holt, J. A. McCauley, W. A. Fogleman, and W. A. Erwin, after some deliberation, chose the name "Burlington."

From 1869 to 1890 the Lutherans were just a mission in this little town and were served successively by the Rev. W. A. Julian, the Rev. Simeon Scherer, the Rev. Whitson Kimball, the Rev. J. L. Buck, R. L. Patterson, C. A. Brown and others, who in large part were theological student supplies for summer vacations, and supervised by visiting pastors as time would permit. This arrangement was maintained until 1890 when the Rev. Charles B. Miller was called as pastor of Macedonia.[13]

The congregation of less than 50 members worshiped in the Union Church building for five years. Under the able leadership of the Rev. Whitson Kimball the congregation raised enough money to build a small church building of frame construction. The building was completed in 1879, and stood on the South side

---

[13]H. P. Wyrick, *A Historical Sketch of Macedonia Lutheran Church,* (Burlington, 1924).

of the railroad about where the W. I. Holt residence was later built and where the Education Building was later built.

With a church building exclusively their own, the Lutherans began to hold services every Sunday, and in 1890 it became a full-fledged member of the Synod. That is to say the church had a resident pastor. It had been a member of the Synod and was known as the "Macedonia Lutheran Church" since April 1869, but was still a mission.

The name "Macedonia" was very appropriately taken from the Bible, The Acts, XVI, 10, which reads: "and when he (Paul) had seen the vision, immediately we sought to go on into Macedonia, concluding that God had called us to preach the gospel to them."

When the chapel was first built, the front entrance was toward Hoke Street. It remained facing Hoke Street until after the summer of 1895, when it was turned around and moved to a lot on Front Street. At that time a parsonage was built which stood at 803 West Front Street until the summer of 1954, although it had been remodeled from time to time.

The Rev. C. B. Miller became pastor in 1890 and served until 1895. During his pastorate the United States was going through what has been called Cleveland's Panic. Collections were light and donations were not so liberal, but the good preacher trusted in the Lord and the Merchants of Burlington trusted him, so, that we may assume that Mr. Miller fared reasonably well during the five years.

Professor J. B. Robertson, who was an authority on the early Lutheran Church, said in his historical account of the Church: "This period from 1869 to 1895 was a period of real struggle and the congregation still numbered less than 50 members."

By 1895 the country was beginning to recover from the panic. Industries of the town were running about normal and more nickels were being dropped in the collection than pennies, and the faithful members of the church were catching up on their contributions to the pastor's salary.

So, the membership grew and quite a few improvements of church property became noticeable. Then the Rev. V. Y. Boozer became pastor. Naturally he lived and worked in much better conditions than his predecessor, the Rev. C. B. Miller.

Mr. Boozer served the church for three years, 1895-1898. This was the most successful period in the church history to this time.

The church building of that time, though small and simple in construction, was quite impressive. It had a small vestibule where the gentlemen of the congregation could leave their hats and overcoats, and the ladies could leave their parasoles or umbrellas.

Pastor Boozer was succeeded in 1898 by the Rev. W. W. J. Ritchie who was the congregations faithful pastor until 1903. During Pastor Ritchie's last year at Macedonia a problem arose which necessitated the calling of a special meeting of the Church Council. The purpose of the meeting was to investigate the trouble between the pastor and Aunt Sue Workman. After the meeting it was decided not to accept the pastor's resignation and to settle the difficulty in a quiet way. It seems the problem arose when Pastor Ritchie, who must have had a special craving for "goobers," decided to plant the entire churchyard in peanuts.[14]

The Rev. C. Brown Cox followed Pastor Ritchie and served the congregation from 1904 to 1912. Pastor Cox was interested and influential in religious and philanthropic movements. He was elected president of the Interdenominational Sunday School Association of North Carolina. "Chiefly through his persistent efforts the Alamance County Ministers' Association was formed, which numbers as its members every active minister in the county, and was and is a power for temperance and righteousness in the county."[15]

In the early part of Pastor Cox's pastorate the congregation declared itself self-supporting for up to this time we had been receiving financial assistance from the North Carolina Synod and the Home Mission Board of the United Lutheran Church South. Times were difficult for the struggling congregation as is evidenced by the fact that it was almost impossible to raise $3 interest on a $50 note. This money was borrowed from one

---

[14]Clemmer, *History of Macedonia Lutheran Church*, p. 4.
[15]*N. C. Sunday School Beacon*, Volume VIII, (Raleigh, N. C., Dec., 1908).

of our members, Isham Ashworth, to help build a barn to house Pastor Cox's horse and it cost the congregation approximately $100. There was much talk about building a new church and at a congregational picnic the subject came up again. The majority of the members said, "We can't build because we are already in debt." Mr. Ashworth reached into his vest pocket, pulled out a slip of paper, struck a match and burned the paper. Then he quietly but firmly remarked, "There's no debt now. Let's build."

So began serious planning for the new church building. The lot now occupied by Strickland Funeral Home, was sold to Mr. George Fogleman for $500. This was the nucleus of the building fund. We can find no record of the cost in dollars and cents of the Sanctuary, but we know that the members used in loving service the talents with which God had endowed them. John A. Bryan was responsible for the brickwork; L. C. Christman assisted by J. J. May and A. C. Mitchel, the woodwork; W. R. Ross after his day's work in the mill came up to the churchyard and made all the cement trim on the building.

The interior furnishings and furnishing were also done by our own members. W. J. Younger made the bulletin boards; Martin Noah built the altar, the pulpit and the chancel and choir railings; and Walter Cheek made the Clergy seats.

All the members, young and old, were given the opportunity to use their money and talents in building this church, and it was completed in 1909.

The Rev. C. I. Morgan came to serve us after Pastor Cox's departure, staying only eleven months. The Rev. T. S. Brown followed the Rev. C. I. Morgan in 1913 and remained until 1922. Those were eventful years. The Synod met with our congregation twice, in 1914 and 1921. The 1914 Synodical meeting was routine, but the meeting in 1921, was historical. In North Carolina there were two Synods, one called the North Carolina Synod and the other the Tennessee Synod. On June 7, 1921, the last meeting of the old North Carolina Synod was held in Front Street Methodist Church, and at the same time a similar meeting was being held by the Tennessee Synod in the Lutheran Church. Upon completion of preliminary business, each Synod adjourned and the N. C. Synodical pastors and delegates marched up the streets to Macedonia Lutheran Church to merge with their sister Synod to form what is now the North Carolina Synod of the Lutheran Church in America.

On two different occasions during Pastor Brown's pastorate, the parsonage caught fire. The first time only the roof was lost and this was quickly replaced. On the other occasion the house was so nearly destroyed that the insurance company declared the building a total loss. This time it was rebuilt and made more modern with two rooms being added. It is supposed that some valuable church records were lost in this second fire.

In 1922 the Rev. H. P. Wyrick accepted the congregational call and served the parish from 1922 to 1930. Burlington was growing and Macedonia grew with it. During his pastorate a new Sunday School Annex was erected, at a cost of $13,000 and substantial repairs made to the Church and the Church property in general. The new Sunday School had a remarkable effect upon the growth of the church. This was due in part to the New Sunday School Building but perhaps more to an awakened interest of the congregation to its obligation to the young life of our own Lutheran homes and the youth of the community.

The Rev. Edward Fulenwider, D. D. began his pastorate January 1, 1930. He led the congregation in substantial growth and progress. The Church grew in membership and through the generosity of Mr. and Mrs. B. V. May additional grounds came to the Church. Records show that 281 members were added to the rolls during his ten years as Pastor.[16]

The first Vacation Bible School was held in 1931 under the supervision of Mrs. B. V. May (Mrs. E. H. Foley). This has become an annual event since that time and almost without exception.

During the 1930's Macedonia did not escape the plight the entire nation was caught up in, that being the "Great Depression." The Church Council was forced to take official action to relieve individual members of their pledged obligations on condition that they make a new pledge and a sincere effort to fulfill it.

On several occasions the church was saved from embarrassment by loans from some of its members. However, by hard and persistent work on the part of dedicated members and the pastor these difficulties were met and the church went forward in the work to which it was appointed.

---

[16]Macedonia Lutheran Church—Seventy-Fifth Anniversary Observance, (Burlington, 1944), p. 4.

In March of 1939, a lot willed to the church by the late Isham Ashworth was sold for $200. Then on May 3, of the same year an announcement was made to the Church Council that Mr. and Mrs. B. V. May had purchased the Green property at the rear of the church on Webb Avenue and were giving it to the Church. A small brick building located on the new property became the home for the newly organized Boy Scout Troop #39. This building has continued to be called the Scout Hut.

Just prior to the arrival of the Rev. L. Boyd Hamm who came to Macedonia in 1940, the congregation bought a new parsonage at a cost of $8,000. The parsonage, which was located five blocks from the church on West Front Street, was used until 1961.

Pastor Hamm's pastorate (1940-1946) was a very active one. This was due in no small part to the vitality which he brought our church, but also the United States was involved in a World War for four of these seven years.

The first Parish Worker employed by the congregation was Miss Elizabeth Petrea. She served for a part of 1941. She left to become the wife of the Rev. Herman Cauble.

The congregation agreed in 1941 to pay a proportionate sum of money in order that the Burlington City Schools might employ a Bible teacher. This has been continued through the years.

In 1942 the Rev. L. David Miller was called as assistant pastor and organist. He remained with us a year and was called as assistant pastor to Holy Trinity Lutheran Church in New York City.

A kindergarten was started at Macedonia in 1943, but had to be closed in 1949. It seems that Macedonia was premature in this area for there was not enough interest to maintain it.

The members of Macedonia did not lack patriotism for during the War many of the congregational sons died in action and many more endured hardships and brought honor to our country, our state, our community, and our church. The ladies of the church also served the patriotic cause. They came to the Sunday School Annex and served for the Red Cross. The women and young people also took their turns in serving at the U. S. O. Center in our City. The grounds to the rear of the church were offered to the C. S. O. for drill exercise on Tuesdays and Thursdays.

Macedonia at one time had the finest playground facilities in this area. The playground was opened in the afternoon to the children of the community. Members of the congregation gave their time and materials for building bowling alleys, shuffle board, tennis courts, and other recreational facilities. Some furnished equipment for playing games such as croquet, badminton, tennis, and others.

The Rev. J. L. Norris and his family came to Macedonia in 1947. His family included three teen-agers which proved to be an inspiration to the young people of the congregation.

On April 3, 1949, at a congregational meeting it was moved that a Building Committee be appointed to secure plans and specifications to be presented to the congregation for ratification. In 1952 plans for the Educational Building were almost complete and early in 1953 the Building Committee (J. M. Bryan, Sr., Myron Rhyne, R. R. Isenhour) had made final corrections. By July 1953, plans had been accepted and contracts awarded for a total of $196,984.00 with the total cost including drainage pipe and ground improvement approximately $207,000.00. The Accumulated Building Fund amounted to $95,166.33. It was on Sunday, July 26, 1953, that the ground was broken for the Educational Building and on June 17, 1954, the building was ready for inspection. Then came the task of the furnishings. The adult classes provided furniture for their classrooms. Many necessary pieces of equipment were given by individuals. Finally everything was ready for occupancy and the formal opening was the first Sunday in August, 1954.

Dr. Norris, at the request of the National Lutheran Council, was granted three months leave of absence in May of 1950 to serve in Europe on the Displaced Persons Program. This was a great honor to both Dr. Norris and the congregation to have been selected for so important a task.

In 1951, A. H. Fogleman, a faithful and devout member, died and left certain monies to establish an aid fund. His will read: "Then after my personal and real property has been disposed of, either by private or public sale, one-tenth of the amount after bills are paid, I bequeath to Macedonia Lutheran Church for a fund to help the poor and distressed, any race or nationality."

Dr. Norris constantly tried to keep the youth interested in the church and its activities. On October 2, 1954, our first Week Day Church School opened. The school has steadily grown and in 1969, 101 were enrolled. At this school, catechetical classes, the church liturgy and other phases of religious education are taught in order that even the very young may participate in the worship service of the church.

In 1956, an amendment was made to the church constitution which permitted women to serve on the Church Council. And for the first time in the history of the church, two ladies, Mrs. E. H. Foley and Mrs. Eva C. Clemmer, were elected to this governing body of our church.

Dr. Norris left us in November, 1957 to accept a call to Grace Lutheran Church in Hendersonville, N. C. and until June 15, 1958, the congregation was without a regular pastor. Thanks to the teachers and students of the Southern Lutheran Theological Seminary of Columbia, South Carolina, we did not miss a Morning Worship Service. This helped to hold the congregation together.

The Rev. W. F. Milholland, a graduate of our Southern Theological Seminary, was called by the congregation. Not having had a pastor fresh from the Seminary since 1895, when the Rev. V. Y. Boozer came, the church hardly knew what to expect. It took little time for activity to begin.

During Pastor Milholland's three year stay at Macedonia many significant things happened. One-hundred and ninety-one new members were received and the debt on the educational building was liquidated. A building committee was set up to begin planning for a new sanctuary. Probably the most significant accomplishment during this period was the beginning of the new mission congregation, Messiah Lutheran Church. Macedonia gave the new church one thousand dollars and transferred forty-four adult members and twenty-two children to Messiah. There were some who were concerned that the new mission would hurt Macedonia, but the opposite proved to be true when both offerings and attendance at Macedonia increased. On August 31, 1961, the Rev. Milholland left Macedonia to accept a call as pastor of Christ Lutheran Church, Roanoke, Virginia.

The Rev. Hoyle L. Whiteside followed the Rev. W. L. Milholland as Pastor of Macedonia. With Pastor Whiteside came his youthful and energetic wife as well as two fine children.

He began his pastorate on October 31, 1961, and not long after their arrival the congregation on November 19, 1961 voted to purchase a new parsonage on 2226 Edgewood Avenue.

On December 16, 1962 the congregation was forced to move from the old church sanctuary into the Sunday School assembly room for Sunday Morning Worship Services due to a furnace breakdown. It was apparent that the congregation would either have to approve major repairs to the old sanctuary or put special emphasis on the efforts of the building committee which had been organized while Rev. Milholland was there to build a new sanctuary. With the vigorous and effective leadership of Pastor Whiteside, Mr. Willis G. Boland, Mr. J. M. Bryan, Sr. and many others it was not long before definite plans were readied for congregational approval. The Carroll property, which adjoined the Church property on Front Street was purchased. This was approved by the congregation on March 24, 1963. The

Picture of 3rd Church Building 1909-1962

19

The cong

n in 1969.

1965

congregation voted unanimously to accept the plans for the new Sanctuary as recommended by the Church Council, and to let the contract for its construction at a called meeting on September 29, 1963. The ground breaking for the new sanctuary was in October 1963, and by February 28, 1965 everything was ready for the Service of Dedication.

The growth of the congregation has been outstanding during the 1960's. The established membership as well as the many new members who have come into the congregation seemed to gain a new vitality. Participation in the many church programs has been very broad.

In September 1967, Mr. William Batterman came to Macedonia as Assistant to the Pastor with primary responsibilities in the area of Youth Work and Christian Education. As a result of Mr. Batterman's work the activities and programs of our youth groups were accelerated to a new level. Mr. Batterman remained at Macedonia until May, 1968 when he accepted a call as pastor to New Covenant Lutheran Church in High Point. He was followed by Mr. Jerry Schumm in September of 1968. Mr. Schumm's official title is Director of Youth Ministry. The efforts of both of these young men have been outstanding. The high point of this activity was the presentation of a folk mass on January 26, 1969.

In June of 1968, the Rev. E. K. Bodie, who had retired from full time ministry came to Macedonia as an Assistant to Pastor Whiteside. His efforts with the older members of our congregation as well as the congregation at large have been very rewarding.

Macedonia has had the rare privilege of having the North Carolina Synod hold two of its annual meetings here in the past four years. The Synod met in May, 1965 at Macedonia for the first time in forty-four years, and again in May, 1969. The 1965 meeting was related to the dedication of our new sanctuary and the 1969 meeting was held at Macedonia in conjunction with the 100th anniversary of the congregation.

Macedonia today is still growing. It still has a healthy concern for the community as well as for itself-displaying that concern through individual services performed by many members of the congregation and its pastor.

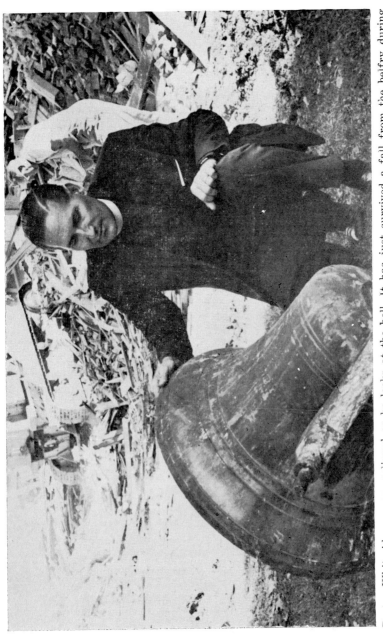

Pastor Whiteside appears relieved as he looks at the bell. It has just survived a fall from the belfry during the destruction of the 2nd Church building.

The church bell was originally purchased by the North Carolina Railway for use in the Union Church. The bell was cast by Henry McShane, Inc. of Baltimore in 1874, and weighs about 700 pounds. When the Union Church building was torn down in 1934 the bell was purchased by the late Ben V. May and the late H. F. Mitchell. Five years later in 1939 the bell was installed at Macedonia. Now, it has been installed into its new mounting in the new sanctuary.

PASTORS

Photo

Not

Available

W. A. Julian

1869-1870

Simeon Scherer

1873-1876

Photo

Not

Available

Whitson Kimball

1876-1880

J. L. Buck

1882-1887

Stu. C. A. Brown

1889

C. B. Miller

1890-1895

V. Y. Boozer

1895-1898

Photo

Not

Available

W. W. J. Ritchie

1898-1903

26

C. B. Cox

1904-1912

C. I. Morgan

1912-1913

T. S. Brown

1913-1922

H. P. Wyrick

1922-1930

Edward Fulenwider   L. Boyd Hamm

1930-1940   1940-1946

J. L. Norris

1947-1957

W. L. Milholland

1958-1961

Hoyle L. Whiteside

1961-

MISS CLEMENTINE SELLARS

Miss Clementine Sellars, affectionately known as "Miss Clem" is the oldest living member of Macedonia Lutheran Church. Daugher of Thomas and Mrs. Margaret Ann Sellars "Miss Clem" was born January 26, 1875 at the homeplace on Union Avenue, Burlington, then known as Company Shops.

"Miss Clem" was baptized by supply Pastor W. B. Cook at Macedonia in October 1888. She is a charter member of Macedonia Lutheran Church Women which was known as Macedonia Woman's Missionary Society when she joined in 1895.
From 1912-1918 "Miss Clem" was employed at the Lutheran Children's Home of the South in Salem, Virginia where she taught sewing to the girls.

For a number of years "Miss Clem" was a Sunday School teacher at Macedonia and was active in all phases of church work.
At the present time "Miss Clem" resides at the North Carolina Lutheran Home in Hickory, North Carolina.

CHURCH COUNCIL

FIRST ROW, Left to Right—Mr. M. A. Boehm, Mr. Kenneth B. Boland, Mrs. Fred E. Fuqua, Mr. George M. Keck, Mr. Wade Dodson, SECOND ROW—Mr. Willis G. Boland, Mr. Joe R. Keenan, Dr. Robert A. Watson, Mr. L. Glenn Ford, Mr. R. Don Russell, Pastor Hoyle L. Whiteside. THIRD ROW—Mr. Roy D. Apple, Mr. Robert A. Lentz, Mr. Amel H. Fuqua, Mr. Floyd Thompson, Mr. Thomas B. DeLoache, Jr., Mr. Donald L. Matkins, Mr. Grover W. Moore, Mr. Boyd L. Black. NOT PICTURED—Dr. Dwight T. Kernodle, Mr. Frederick J. Sternberg, Mr. Carl F. Turbyfill.

31

ROLL OF MEMBERS

Adams, Roy C.
 Mrs. Roy (Jean Paula)
 Kurt Luke, Joel Young
Aldridge, William
 Mrs. William (Anne)
 Anne, Janet
Allred, Alvin, Jr.
 Mrs. Alvin, Jr. (Juanita)
 Richie Lee, Wayne, Joel Edward,
 Sandra Lynn, Patty,
 Bryon Douglas
Allred, Alvin, Sr.
 Mrs. Alvin, Sr. (Catherine)
Allred, Mrs. Mark (Nancy Lashley)
 Laurie Marie
Apple, Mrs. Leonard (Carol)
 Sharon Lynn, Nancy Carol
Apple, Roy D.
 Mrs. Roy D. (Evelyn)
 William, John Mark, David,
 Robert, Daniel
Bailey, R. Oscar
Baldwin, Mrs. Berta Mae
 Ernie, Franklin
Baldwin, Thomas
Barnes, Carroll Eric
Barnes, Rickey
 Mrs. Rickey (Ellen Keenan)
Barnes, William Allen
 Mrs. William (Ellen)
 Kathryn Ann, Karen Lynn
Barneycastle, Mrs. A. E. (Alvania)
Barringer, Dwight R.
 Mrs. Dwight R. (Cleo)
 Mary Joyce
Beckom, Mrs. Elaine
Beckom, J. D.
Bendigo, E. I.
 Mrs. E. I. (Mae)
Bevan, Mrs. R. D., Jr. (Helen)
 Robert Douglas, III
Bivens, Thomas Alton
 Mrs. T. A. (Charlotte)
 Kenneth Alton, Charlotte Ann
Bjerk, Mrs. Edward (Ella)
Black, Boyd Lee
 Mrs. Boyd Lee (Betsy)
 Lawrence, Frederick William,
 Samuel
Black, Ellon B.
 Mrs. Ellon (Elizabeth)
 William B., Katherine Jane,
 Robert Ellon, Judith Loraine,
 Cynthia Ann
Black, Paul R.
 Mrs. Paul R. (Thames)
 Mickey
Black, Mrs. Zelma

Black, Mrs. Howard T. (Marie)
 Carman, Howard, Jr.
Bodie, Rev. Earl K.
 Mrs. Earl (Annie Belle)
Boehm, M. A. (Bud)
 Mrs. M. A. (Polly)
Boland, Jrs. C. J. (Mamie)
Boland, Carlton Brown
 Mrs. Carlton (Polly)
 Linda Diane, Carlton, Jr.
Boland, Kenneth B.
 Mrs. Kenneth (Geneva)
 Jeanette, Charles, Angela
Boland, W. D.
 Mrs. W. D. (Lottie)
Boland, Willis Grey
 Mrs. Willis (Christine)
Boley, Harry P., Jr.
 Mrs. Harry P., Jr. (Barbara)
 Michael, Jean Marie
Bond, Howard
 Mrs. Howard (Ruth)
 Jeffrey, Roger, Diane
Boone, Mrs. C. H. (Frances)
Bost, E. L.
 Maude
Bowman, Russell, L.
 Mrs. R. L. (Johnsie)
Brendle, Ronnie A.
 Mrs. Ronnie (Diane)
 Chalese Dawn
Brooks, Robert
 Mrs. Robert (Virginia)
 Susan
Brown, James Gilbert
 Mrs. James (Peggy)
 James Gilbert, II
Bryan, Curry E., Jr.
 Mrs. Curry E. (Irma)
 Leigh, Billy, Curry, II,
 Martha Hope
Bryan, Jennings M., Jr.
 Mrs. Jennings M., Jr. (Eloise)
 J. M., III
Bryan, Mrs. Jennings, Sr. (Letha)
Bryan, Richard H.
 Mrs. Richard H. (Ila)
 Richard, David H., Jo Anna
Bryant, George Arlen
 Mrs. George Arlen (Janice)
 Robert Arlen, David Michael,
 Daniel Mark, John Ross
Bryan, Mrs. Worth (Grace)
Bryan, William B.
 Mrs. William B. (Ann)
 John
Burgess, Chester Walton, III
 Mrs. Chester W. (Becky)

Byers, Cheryle
Byers, Leonard Wayne
Mrs. L. Wayne (Nancy)
Campbell, Mrs. Brenda
Lowell Todd
Castagna, Mrs. Sam (Billie)
Samuel Nathan, Anthony Correll
Carter, Mrs. Quincey A., Sr.
(Janie LaVinnie)
Chance, Charles, Jr.
Mrs. Charles, Jr. (Vickie)
Crystalynne Michelle
Chance, Mrs. Charles, Sr. (Winnie)
Mary Lynn
Clemmer, Mrs. Eva
Clemmer, Lewis C.
Mrs. Lewis (Pearl)
Louise, Lawrence, Eva
Cobb, Coy
Mrs. Coy (Beulah)
Cobb, Paul E.
Mrs. Paul (Elizabeth)
Richard
Cobb, Paul E., Jr.
Coble, Henry Clay
Mrs. Henry Clay (Bernice)
Frederick Cyrus
Coble, Wade
Mrs. Wade (Agnes)
Coble, Worth D.
Mrs. Worth (Geneva)
Chambers, Harry T.
Mrs. Harry T. (Shirley)
Carlee Howell, Dolly
Coley, Mrs. W. L. (Ollie)
Conatser, Derek
Kathryn LeAnne
Copland, James R., Jr.
Mrs. J. R., Jr. (Lilliam)
Copland, J. R., III
Mrs. J. R., III (Harriett)
Copland, Ronald
Mrs. Ronald (Sharon)
Catherine Paige
Cox, Alan
Mrs. Alan (Barbara)
William Alan, Patrick Leland
Coyner, E. Harper
Mrs. E. Harper (Ruth)
Crabill, Mrs. C. Clark (Edna)
Cynthia Ann
Cepas, Mrs. K. V. (Lidija)
Crane, Mrs. Anne
William Benjamin, Tom
Creech, Mrs. Kermit (Blanche)
Carol
Crumpler, John
Mrs. John (Rena)
John Christopher, Gregory

Crowson, Paul F.
Mrs. Paul F. (Clara)
Danna Farrar
Curry, James
Mrs. James (Eva)
Dahl, Ernest B.
Mrs. Ernest B. (Ollie)
Ernest Byron, David DeMoss
Darlington, Fred, III
Mrs. Fred (Vicki)
Julia Collins
Davis, Jrs. Carl (Tut)
Sandra, Theresa
Davis, Fred Y.
Mrs. Fred (Carol)
Monica Lynnette
Davis, Mrs. Ruth
DeLoache, T. B., Jr.
Mrs. T. B., Jr. (Sara)
T. B., III, Nancy Pollack, George
DeLoache, Mrs. T. B., Sr. (Julia)
Devoe, Mrs. Amherst
Dillberger, Edward
Mrs. Edward (Elaine)
John Edward, Robert
Dodson, Wade E.
Mrs. Wade E. (Louise)
Richard K. Sharpe
Dunn, Mrs. Esther
DuPree, Mrs. John P. (Helen Buff)
DeBoard, Charles Lacy
Mrs. Charles L. (Pat)
Maria Gayle, Craig Young
Earnhardt, John
Mrs. John (Jean)
David Chandler, Philip Andrews
Edwards, John William
Edwards, Mrs. Margaret G.
Edwards, Col. Raymond F.
Mrs. Raymond F. (Elma)
Faggart, R. L.
Mrs. R. L. (Ann)
Ferrell, Mrs. Robert E. (Jane)
Ferrell, Kenneth
Mrs. Kenneth (Faye)
Lisa Carol
File, M. L.
Fogleman, A. Brown
Mrs. A. Brown (Gwendolyn)
Donald
Fogleman, Hal Morton
Mrs. Hal (Ruth)
Fogleman, John P.
Mrs. John P. (Savannah)
Fogleman, Joseph H.
Mrs. Joseph H. (Dorothy)
Harold Lee
Foley, Mrs. E. H. (Louise)
Ford, Harold Grant

33

Ford, L. Glenn
  Mrs. L. Glenn (Lelia)
  Christine, Lee, Craven
Frye, Mrs. J. L.
Fuqua, Amel H.
  Mrs. Amel H. (Grethel)
Fuqua, Fred E.
  Mrs. Fred (Edna)
  Ladd, Fredda
Fuqua, Larry W.
  Mrs. Larry W. (Rebecca)
  Alice Dunn
Fuqua, Mrs. Neita
Gaston, John T.
  Mrs. John T. (Helen)
  Patricia Diane, Katherine, Sandra
Gee, Wallace W.
  Mrs. Wallace (Edna Pearl)
  John Franklin
Gentry, Herbert
  Mrs. Herbert (Katherine)
  Larry Wayne
Gilliam, Don
  Mrs. Don (Rozanne)
  Kimberly Paige
Gilliam, John J.
  Mrs. John J. (Hilda)
  John Jacob, Jr., Jesse Kingsland
Gladden, Gene
Glenn, Ross W.
  Mrs. Ross W. (Allie)
Goodman, Clyde
  Dale McIver
Graves, Mrs. C. L. (Sarah)
Graves, James H., Jr.
  Mrs. James H., Jr. (Katherine)
  Katherine Jennifer
Graves, J. Harold, Sr.
  Mrs. J. Harold (Jackie)
Greene, Lloyd C.
Gruenhagen, James
  Mrs. James (Pat)
Hahn, Arlie Alexander
  Mrs. Arlie A. (Alda)
  Barbara, Arlie, Jr.
Hall, Anthony (Tony)
  Mrs. Anthony (Martha Jo)
  Charles Daniel
Haney, Charles
  Mrs. Charles (Katherine)
  Ibby
Halbert, Mrs. W. S. (Kay)
Harless, Jack L.
  Mrs. Jack (Joyce)
  Jeremy Leland
Hansen, Thomas A.
  Mrs. Thomas A. (Betty)
  Tommy, Jr., Sheryle Lynn,
  Kenneth Michael
Harris, Charles Ralph
  Mrs. Charles (Sylvia)
  Loria Ann

Hatley, James H.
  Mrs. James H. (Sadie)
  Karen James H., III
Haynes, Mrs. W. W. (Frances)
Heritage, Mrs. James H. (Eileen)
Hiller, Kermit E.
  Mrs. Kermit E. (Beverly)
  Dennis Edward, Deborah, Denise
Hallsey, Jim B. (Mrs.)
Hines, James
  Mrs. James (Betty)
  Deborah, Jimmy
Heilig, Harry Brown
  Mrs. Harry (Eunice)
  Lisa Ann, Jeffrey Neil
Hodges, Mrs. David (Barbara)
Holt, Mrs. D. C. (Irene)
Holt, Daniel Lewis
  Mrs. Daniel Lewis (Rachel)
Holt, Roger M.
  Mrs. Roger (Martha)
  Rodney Monroe, Bruce, Phyliss
Hooper, Fred Veach
Hopkins, David C.
Hopkins, Grover Lewis, Jr.
  Mrs. Grover L. (Betty)
Hopkins, Mrs. Grover L., Sr.
  (Dessie)
Hopkins, Bennie Lee
  Mrs. Bennie (Ann)
Hopkins, Mark Lewis
  Mrs. Mark (Vivian)
  Clifton Ray, Kenneth,
  Mark Lewis, Jr., Cynthia,
  Vivian Ann, Earl
Hopkins, Orbin C.
  Mrs. Orbin C. (Mattie)
Horne, S. Allen
  Mrs. S. Allen (Dollie)
Horner, Mrs. Hadley (Louise)
  Patricia Ann, Elizabeth Louise,
  Jr., Elizabeth Brent
Horner, Mrs. Martin, Sr. (Emily)
  Martin, E., Jr.
Hunley, J. Henry
  Mrs. J. Henry (Alice)
  Randy Michael
Irwin, Richard
  Mrs. Richard (Linda)
  Robert Brittain
Isley, Mrs. C. Ray (Bonnie)
Isley, Michael M.
  Mrs. M. M. (Sara)
Isley, Phillip L.
  Mrs. Phillip L. (Drusilla)
Isley, W. K.
  Mrs. W. K. (Ruth)
Isley, Billy Martin
  Mrs. Billy (Frankie)
Jefferies, William N.
  Mrs. William N. (Sarah)
  William T.

Jeffcoat, Lloyd E.
Jenkins, F. Alfred
  Mrs. F. Alfred (Alice)
Jensen, Eric
  Mrs. Eric (Amanda)
  Karen Edith, John Eric
Johnson, Donald L.
  Mrs. Donald L. (Nancy)
  Lorimer Anne, Christie Leigh
Johnson, Donald E.
  Mrs. Donald (Sylvia)
  Cynthia Gray, Donald Wayne
Johnson, Lester
  Mrs. Lester (Betty)
  Meredith, Christine, Marjorie
Jones, C. Macon
  Mrs. C. Macon (Elizabeth)
  Kenneth, Thomas E.
Kanipe, Lloyd Alfred
  Mrs. Lloyd (Judy)
  Lanya Michelle
Keck, George M.
  Mrs. George (Geneva)
  George Arnold
Keenan, Joe R.
  Mrs. Joe R. (Dorothy)
  Susan
Keller, Mrs. Henry F. (Virginia)
Kernodle, Dr. Dwight Talmadge
  Mrs. Dwight (Grace)
  Dwight, Jr., Jane Harriet,
  Ann Grace
Ketner, Dr. Calvin L.
  Mrs. Calvin L. (Lucille)
Ketner, Cletus J.
  Mrs. Cletus J. (Harriet)
Ketner, Walter Jack
  Mrs. W. Jack (Hilda)
  Cynthia, Jack
Kilpatrick, Glenn
  Mrs. Glenn (Faye)
  David Paul
Kimbro, Mrs. Norene
King, Charles Edwin
  Mrs. Edwin (Mary Lee)
  Charles Edwin, II
Kingsmore, Harry
Kivett, Mrs. T. H. (Lorah)
Kock, Charles J., Jr.
Lail, Fred R.
  Mrs. Fred (Martha)
  Fred, Jr.
Ledbetter, Louis Richard
  Mrs. Louis Richard (Judith Gail)
  Christina Marie, Suzanne Dee
Lentz, Robert A.
  Mrs. Robert (Betty)
  Ann, Robert, Sue
Leonard, Mrs. C. A. (Gladys)
Lindsey, Carl
Lookabill, Miss Odessa
Loy, Mrs. Charles W.

Martin, Charles Eugene
  Mrs. C. Eugene (Carolyn)
  Liza, Pete, Kirk, Joe
Martin, R. P.
  Mrs. R. P. (Carole)
  Teresa Ann, Gregory Lee
Masten, Henry
  Mrs. Henry (Martha)
Matkins, Donald L.
  Mrs. Donald (Ruth Whittecar)
May, D. Eugene
May, Emanuel, Jr.
  Mrs. Emanuel (Rachel)
May, Emanuel, III
  Mrs. Emanuel, III (Diane)
May, W. W.
Meachem, J. Manley
  Mrs. J. Manley (Trudie)
  Johnny
Mebane, Mrs. W. W. (Margaret)
  Miss Nina L.
Metts, Mrs. Carey G, III
McAllister, Larry B.
  Mrs. Larry B. (Edna)
  Larry Bikle, Jr., Thomas Frank,
  Barbara Ann
McCauley, Mrs. O. W. (Irene)
McClintock, Mrs. Charles (Barbara)
  Beverly, Ada Richy, Charles, Jr.
McKeel, Miss Beulah
McKeon, Mrs. Jack (Carol Jean)
McKinney, Joseph A.
  Mrs. Joe (Rita)
  Christopher
McNair, Mrs. Patricia
  Kathleen Lynn, Bill, Mike, David
McPherson, William King
  Mrs. William K. (Ingrid)
  Michelle Rosa
Miller, William R.
  Mrs. Bill (Marie)
  Thomas, Patricia, Christine
Mitchell, H. F., Jr.
  Mrs. H. F., Jr. (Ruth)
  Lea
Mitchell, James Clair
  James Clair, III
Moehring, Paul A.
  Mrs. Paul A. (Miriam)
  Janice Ellen, John Christian,
  Kenneth Allen
Moore, G. William
  Mrs. G. William (Jane)
  Julia Elizabeth, Grover W., Jr.,
  Susan Willis
Moore, Miss Catherine Willis
Moore, Miss Mamie
Moore, R. Keith
  Mrs. R. Keith (Kathryn)
  R. Keith, Jr.
Moore, Zeb V.
  Mrs. Zeb V. (Ola)
  Aaron, David, Linda

Moser, Miss Anne D.
  Miss Sallie
Murray, Edward L.
  Mrs. Edward L. (Edna)
  Tommy, Lane
Murray, Dr. Henry V., Sr.
  Mrs. Henry V. (Maude)
Murrie, Ira C.
  Mrs. Ira C. (Lottie)
Newton, Milton G.
  Mrs. Milton (Molly)
  Steve
Needham, Mrs. Mathom, Jr.
  (Elizabeth)
Norcom, Charlie W., Jr.
  Mrs. Charlie W. (Sarah)
  Mary Ann
Owen, Lacy B., Jr.
  Mrs. Lacy B., Jr. (Jane)
  John Alan, Lee Ann
Paige, Ronnie
Patton, Daniel C.
  Mrs. Daniel C. (Violet)
  Danny, Denise Carolyn, Cheryl
Patton, Mrs. J. D. (Annie)
Pennington, Carlos A.
  Mrs. Carlos A. (Smithy)
  Daniel Worth, Carlos Bryan
Perry, W. M.
  Mrs. W. M. (Lois)
Peterson, Grady F.
  Mrs. Grady F. (Imogene)
  Grady Fuqua, Catherine Lynn
Petrea, Luke P.
  Mrs. Luke P. (Raymelle)
Phillips, Moody
  Mrs. Moody (Myra)
Pickard, Charles F.
  Mrs. Charles F. (Elizabeth)
Poovey, William A.
  Mrs. William A. (Mamie)
Poovey, William P.
  Mrs. William (Patricia)
  Robert Alan, Jennifer Lynn,
  Karen Elizabeth
Pardue, David E., Jr.
  Mrs. David E. (Rebecca)
  David E., III
Pittard, Mrs. David (Nancy)
  Michael David, Jr.
Ray, Mrs. Malon P. (Doris)
Ray, James M.
  Mrs. James M. (Bette)
  Tammy Suzanne
Reinhardt, Ned E.
  Mrs. Ned (Ruth)
  Christy Dawn, Neal Alan
Reinke, John H.
  Mrs. John H. (Norma)
  Dawn, Karen Gay, Panela
Reitzel, Miss Blanche C.
Reitzel, Virgil Y.

Renegar, Richard G.
  Mrs. Richard (Linda)
Rethaford, Willis
  Mrs. Willis (Rebecca)
  Michele Lynn
Rhyne, Myron
  Mrs. Myron (Sarah)
  Sarah Janet
Rhodes, Elbert F.
  Mrs. Elbert F. (Lorene)
Rhodes, Franklin P.
  Mrs. Franklin (Grace)
  Barbara Ann, Robert, Gail
Rick, Carl W., Jr.
Riddle, Egbert A.
  Mrs. Egbert A. (Lavie)
Roensch, A. O. (Dick)
  Mrs. A. O. (Jean)
  Rhonda Lea
Rowe, Mrs. Robert A. (Pearl)
Royster, Mrs. W. F. (Sadie)
Rudd, Mrs. Frank P. (Flossie)
  Helen
Rudisill, Michael E.
  Mrs. Michael E. (Theo)
  (Martin) Henry, Theo (Frazier),
  (John) Roland, Virginia (Yvonne)
Russell, Donald
  Mrs. Donald (Jane)
  Douglas Page, Andrew Gordon
Scott, H. Edwin
  Mrs. H. Edwin (Bertha)
  Tony
Schulz, Paul Martin, Jr.
  Mrs. Paul M. (Ellen)
  Eric Davis
Scott, Eddie Wayne
Sharpe, Adrian
Sharpe, Roy H.
  Mrs. Roy H. (Barbara)
  Cynthia Ellen, Karen Lynne
Shoffner, Mrs. Jesse (Maggie)
Shoffner, Joseph E.
  Mrs. Joseph (Ola)
  Joseph E., Jr.
Simpson, Mrs. W. M. (Virginia)
Sloop, Larry E.
  Mrs. Larry E. (Judy)
  Wendy, Kevan
Smith, Mrs. Stan (Linda)
  Tammy René
Snyder, Calvin
  Mrs. Calvin (Janet)
  David Lee, Robert Edward,
  Howard James, Terry Jo,
  Lynn Marie, Tracy Jean,
  William Thomas
Starr, Mrs. Donald (Dorothy)
  John Arthur, Michael Dale
Steele, Kenneth L.
  Miss Nellie G.

Sternberg, Frederick
  Mrs. Frederick (Elizabeth)
  Scott Frederick, Tracy Elizabeth
Stone, Hoyte Eday
  Hoyte E., Jr., Barry Edward
Stousland, Olav
  Mrs. Olav (Rachel)
  Williamson, Tommy, Neal
Strange, Mrs. C. Gilbert (Helen)
Stuber, Clarence A.
  Mrs. Clarence A. (Genevieve)
  Stephen Lynn, Sharon Kay,
  Ronald Dean
Sullivan, James V.
  Mrs. James V. (Beulah)
Sumner, Herbert W.
  Mrs. Herbert W. (Frances)
  Stephen Wayne
Thomas, Mrs. Richard (Mildred)
Thompson, Floyd V.
  Mrs. Floyd V. (Estelle)
  William H.
Thompson, Forris
  Mrs. Forris (Judy)
  Gary, Timothy, Harold
Thompson, Kent B.
Tickle, Dwight D.
  Mrs. Dwight D. (Beulah)
Tickle, Mrs. Alyse
  Gary
Tickle, James V., Sr.
  Mrs. James V., Sr. (Lutie)
Tolley, Jerry R.
  Mrs. Jerry (Joan)
Travis, George
Trollinger, William H.
Troutman, Hanson D.
  Mrs. Hanson D. (Peggy)
  Eleanor, Eric
Turbyfill, Carl
  Mrs. Carl (Kathleen)
  Barbara, Kenneth Dean
Turner, George A.
  Mrs. George A. (Jewel)
  Tommy Allen, Panela,
  Danny Milton
Van Fleet, Lester Gene
  Mrs. L. G. (Linda)
  Darryl Gene, Danny Craig
Walker, Dr. John B., Jr.
  Mrs. John B., Jr. (Piggi)
  John Barrett, III,
  Patricia Ruth (Patty)
Walker, Michael H. (Mickey)
  Mrs. Mickey (GG)
Wallace, Norman H.
Warschkow, Fritz
  Mrs. Fritz (Ingeborg)
  Philip, Heide
Watson, Dr. Robert
  Mrs. Robert (Sue)

Jane Lee, Whitney McRee,
  Kimberly Sue
Way, G. Winfred, Sr. (Doots)
  Mrs. G. W. (Pearl)
  George W., Jr., Sylvia
Wells, Charles H.
  Mrs. Charles H. (Sylvia)
Whiteside, Rev. Hoyle L.
  Mrs. Hoyle L. (Anne)
  Susan Rebekah, Hoyle Lee, Jr.
Williams, Clyde F.
  Mrs. Clyde F. (Ruth)
  Donald, Richard Michael
Willis, Mrs. H. H. (Betsy)
  Susan Beth, David
Wilson, M. Joel
  Mrs. M. Joel (Barbara)
Wolfe, Mrs. J. Donald (Mary Ella)
Wolfgang, Will W.
  Mrs. Will (Jane)
  Bonnie Beth
Woodruff, John
  Mrs. John (Josephine)
  Josephine, Angela
Woody, Robert R.
  Mrs. Robert R. (Helen)
  Frances Ann
Workman, Mrs. Dennis
  (Barbara Turbyfill)
Wray, Wade N.
  Mrs. Wade N. (Nadine)
  Jack
Young, L. I.
  Mrs. L. I. (Maude)
Younger, Mrs. Louise

NON-RESIDENT MEMBERS

Benson, Mrs. C. Kenneth
  (Ann Dahl)
Black, William David
Bjerk, Dr. Edward M.
Bowman, Mrs. Michael (Sue Isley)
Bowman, William Russell
Byrd, Sergeant Carl
  Mrs. Carl (Patsy)
Collier, Mrs. John (Judy Jones)
Copenhaver, Donald E.
  Mrs. Donald E. (Mary Lou)
  Mark Anthony, Lisa Michele
Crane, Miss Barbara
Cripps, Mrs. Ellen
Crouse, Floyd, Jr.
Crumpton, Danny Lee
  Mrs. Danny Lee (John Turner)
Curry, James, Jr.
DeVoto, Mrs. Charles H.
  (Gayle Isley)
Edwards, John W., Jr.
  Mrs. J. W., Jr. (Ellen Abigail)
Edwards, William, Jr.
  Mrs. William B.
  (Theressa McGee)
Emerson, Mrs. James
  (Donna Dunn)
Fagg, Harvey E.
  Mrs. Harvey E. (Eunice)
  Rebecca Gail, Karen Joyce,
  Sarah Jane, Robert Henry,
  Michael
Fogleman, Jon
  Mrs. Jon (Diane Dixon)
Fuqua, Jerry H.
Gee, Charles Daniel
Gee, James Thomas
Gee, William David
  Mrs. W. D. (Kay)
Hayden, Mrs. Joseph W.
Hunley, J. Ronald
  Mrs. J. Ronald (Jean)
  Kim Leigh, Kelli Layne,
  Kris Lynne, James Ronald, Jr.

Keenan, Robert M.
Kirkman, Clyde W.
  Mrs. Clyde (Carolyn)
  Mary Lenora, Clyde Wayne, Jr.,
  Tammy Lynn
Koch, Mr. Charles J., Jr.
Koppell, Hans
  Mrs. Hans
  Heli Sylvia
Lorimer, William H., Jr.
  Mrs. William H., Jr.
Matkins, Mrs. James
  (Peggy Ann Barringer)
May, Benjamin V.
  Mrs. Benjamin (Anne Dickson)
May, Liss Lula
May, Ward
  Mrs. Ward (Ellen)
Mitchell, Bennet M.
Mundy, Steve Darrell
  Mrs. Steve D. (Sandra)
Moiz, Miss Sarah May
Peterson, Dr. Tommy M.
  Mrs. Tommy (Alicia)
Rhodes, Charles R.
Rick, Carl W., Jr.
Ritter, Mrs. Rebecca DeLoache
Rouse, Mrs. T. J. (Ruth)
Russell, Mrs. William W.
  (Vicki Baldwin)
Schaupp, Mrs. John C.
  (Barbara Porter)
Sellers, Miss Clem
Slaughter, Mrs. Catherine
  Laura, Pamela Gwyn
Strange, Charles G., Jr.
  Charles Gilbert, III
Thompson, Vernon
Tripp, Larry D.
Turbyfill, Donald
Wyrick, Granville G.
York, Ross
Younger, Ralph Kendall
Younger, William B.

BIBLIOGRAPHY

Blackwelder, Ruth, *The Age of Orange.* Charlotte Heritage Printers, 1961.

Clemmer, Eva Christman, *History of Macedonia Lutheran Church.* Burlington, 1959.

Documents of the North Carolina Legislature. Raleigh, 1866.

Burlington Times News, March 29, 1956.

Macedonia Lutheran Church—Seventy-Fifth Anniversary Observance. Burlington, 1944.

North Carolina Sunday School Beacon. Vol. VIII, Raleigh, 1908.

Smyth, John F. D., *A Tour in the United States of America.* 2 vols. Dublin: G. Perrin, 1784.

Stockard, Sallie Walker, *The History of Alamance County.* Raleigh: Capital Printing Company, 1900.

Whitaker, Walker, *Centennial History of Alamance County.*

Wyrick, H. P., *A Historical Sketch of Macedonia Lutheran Church.* Burlington, 1924.

Alamance Printing Company, Burlington, N. C.